Ponds

Louise and Richard Spilsbury

Heinemann
LIBRARY

H www.heinemann.co.uk
Visit our website to find out more information about Heinemann Library books.

To order:
☎ Phone 44 (0) 1865 888066
📄 Send a fax to 44 (0) 1865 314091
💻 Visit the Heinemann Bookshop at www.heinemann.co.uk to browse our catalogue and order online.

First published in Great Britain by Heinemann Library,
Halley Court, Jordan Hill, Oxford OX2 8EJ
a division of Reed Educational and Professional Publishing Ltd.
Heinemann is a registered trademark of Reed Educational & Professional Publishing Ltd.

OXFORD MELBOURNE AUCKLAND JOHANNESBURG BLANTYRE
GABORONE IBADAN PORTSMOUTH (NH) USA CHICAGO

Designed by Celia Floyd
Illustrations by Alan Fraser
Originated by Dot Gradations
Printed in Hong Kong/China

ISBN 0 431 03905 4 (hardback)   ISBN 0 431 03912 7 (paperback)
06 05 04 03 02 01   06 05 04 03 02 01
10 9 8 7 6 5 4 3 2   10 9 8 7 6 5 4 3 2 1

British Library Cataloguing in Publication Data
Spilsbury, Louise
    Ponds. – (Wild Britain)
    1. Pond ecology – Great Britain – Juvenile literature
    2. Pond animals – Great Britain – Juvenile literature
    I. Title II. Spilsbury, Richard
    577.6'3

Acknowledgements

To our own young wildlife enthusiasts, Miles and Harriet.

The Publishers would like to thank the following for permission to reproduce photographs:
Bruce Coleman: Sir Jeremy Grayson p5, William S Paton p9, Bob Glover p11, Kim Taylor pp15, 16, 18, George McCarthy p26; Corbis: London Aerial Photo Library p4, Eric Crichton p10; Garden & Wildlife Matters: Jeremy Hoare p6, p28; NHPA: Laurie Campbell p27; Oxford Scientific Films: Mike Slater p7, Harold Taylor p8, Raymond Blythe p12, Fredrik Ehrenstrom p13, Gerald Thompson p14, London Scientific Films pp17, 21b, G I Bernard pp19, 29, David Thompson pp20, 22, Colin Milkins p23, David and Sue Cayless p24, Mike Birkhead p25

Cover photograph reproduced with permission of Oxford Scientific Films

Our thanks to Andrew Solway for his comments in the preparation of this book.

Contents

Any words appearing in the text in bold, **like this**, are explained in the Glossary.

What is a pond?

Ponds can be small, in gardens, or big, as in this park.

A pond is an area of fresh water.
The water in a pond is always still,
unlike water in a river or stream that
is always moving.

4

A pond habitat provides living things, like these ducks, with food, water and **shelter**.

A **habitat** is the natural home of a group of plants and animals. In this book we look at some of the plants and animals that live, grow and **reproduce** in a pond habitat.

5

Types of pond

This city pond is well cared for and many people visit.

Some ponds are made by people. Some are made for a special purpose, such as for cows to drink or fish to **breed** in. Others are made for people to enjoy visiting.

If left alone, this moorland pond may fill with plants or soil, or simply dry up.

Other ponds form naturally in hollows and ditches that fill with rainwater or melting snow. **Seeds** of wild plants blow into the ponds and grow into new plants.

 Changes

Although this pond looks quiet, it is full of life beneath the surface of the water.

In summer ponds are full of life. **Insects,** such as bees, come to feed on the flowering plants. Other animals, like fish, frogs and toads, feed on the insects.

In winter ponds may freeze and turn to ice. This makes it hard for birds to find food.

In winter some plants and animals that live on the surface of ponds sink to the bottom and **hibernate**. Fewer birds and animals may visit the pond because there is little food there for them to eat.

9

Living there

Plants grow in all parts of a pond both in and around it.

The edge of most ponds is quite shallow. Ponds are deeper in the middle. Some plants grow in the shallow water, some on the surface of the water and some under the water.

The edge of a pond provides food and water for many living things, including this turtle dove.

The pond is an ideal **habitat** for many animals. There is water to drink and the plants at the edge provide **shelter**. Birds go there to eat plants, **insects** and fish.

11

Reeds and waterlilies

The **seeds** to grow new reedmace plants, like these, are made in the large flower head at the top.

At the edge of a pond, plants that like shallow water grow. The great reedmace is tall with long underground **stems**. The stems hold the plant up.

The leaves of the yellow waterlily rest above the water to reach the sunlight.

The yellow waterlily has soft, air-filled stems. The water holds up these light stems and the flat leaves rest on the water. Its **roots** are buried in the ground.

13

Water soldiers and milfoils

The water soldier plant floats on top of the water.

Some plants float with their **roots** trailing in the water, instead of being buried in the ground. They get the **nutrients** they need to live and grow from the water.

The milfoil has roots in the ground and flowers above the water.

Some pond plants have their roots in the ground. They take in nutrients from the soil. Their flower heads peep above the surface of the water to reach the sunlight.

Surface insects

Damselflies, like these, can fly very fast to catch their food.

Some **insects** fly above the water. Damselflies and dragonflies have two pairs of wings. They fly over ponds and use their huge eyes to spot tiny insects to eat.

A pond skater catches tiny insects on the water surface.

Some insects can walk on water. They are
so light they can skate across the surface.
A pond skater moves very rapidly this way.

Underwater insects

The water boatman swims using its oar-like legs.

Some **insects** catch their food under the water. The water boatman carries bubbles of air underwater so it can breathe. It returns to the surface of the water for more air when it runs out.

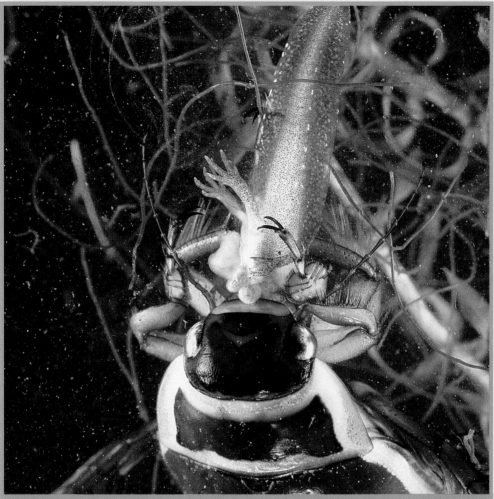
This great diving beetle is eating a tadpole the same size as itself!

The great diving beetle swims underwater to catch food like tiny fish. It moves quickly to catch its food in its strong mouth.

Frogs and tadpoles

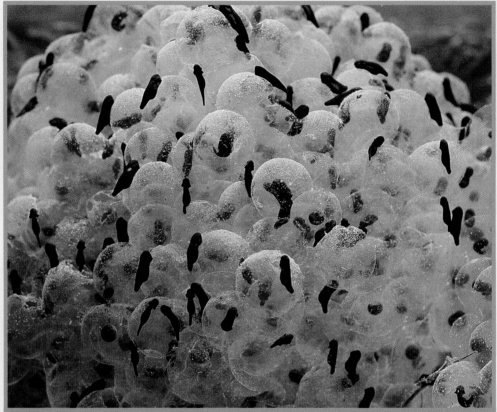

When tadpoles **hatch** out of the frogs' eggs, they feed on tiny water plants.

Frogs are amphibians. This means they start life in the water, but can live on land when fully grown. Female frogs lay hundreds of eggs in water.

The way a tadpole changes into a frog is called metamorphosis.

As the tadpole grows, its body changes. It develops lungs so it can breathe on land, and legs so it can walk. It begins to eat small water animals.

Fish

The male stickleback builds a nest using plants and stones.

Most fish **reproduce** by laying eggs. The female stickleback lays her eggs in a nest built by the male. When the young **hatch** out, the male watches over them until they can look after themselves.

This pike hides in plants at the edge of the pond and darts out suddenly to catch its food.

Pond fish eat all sorts of food, including plants, snails, worms, **insects** and other fish. The pike eats frogs, young birds and fish with its sharp teeth.

Swans and ducks

The swan's long neck helps it reach plants under the water.

Many pond birds, like mallards, geese and swans, have **webbed feet**. This helps them to swim. They feed mostly on grass and water plants from the pond.

Tufted ducks can dive down one or two metres deep.

Tufted ducks feed on underwater plants.
They bite off pieces of the plants that grow
on the bottom of the pond. They also catch
living things like **insects** and small fish to eat.

Coots and herons

A coot watches over its chicks at the edge of a pond.

Coots are mainly black with a white beak and very big feet. Their big feet are for swimming and for tramping across pondweed to find water plants to eat.

The heron is feeding its young with food it has caught and held in its beak.

Herons make nests in trees above the pond. To feed, a heron stands quite still watching the water. Then it suddenly stabs its knife-like beak into the water to catch fish and frogs.

Dangers

This pond is being taken over by soil and plants. When it is gone, the animals that live there will lose their home.

Some ponds dry up naturally. But others are filled with soil or rubbish by people. When ponds are destroyed, plants and animals lose their **habitat**.

Litter has spoilt this pond for everyone.

Litter makes ponds look horrible and it also harms living things. Animals may get trapped inside old tins or containers. Fish and pond plants may die if their water becomes **polluted**.

Food chains

All plants and animals in a pond **habitat** are linked through the food they eat. Food chains show how different living things are linked. Here is one example.

The heron eats the pike.

The pike eats the frog.

The frog eats the water boatman.

The water boatman eats tadpoles.

The artwork on this page is not to scale.

Glossary

breed to have young and increase in number

habitat the natural home of a group of plants and animals

hatch to be born from an egg

hibernate when living things rest in a safe place through winter when it is cold and there is little food about

insects six-legged minibeasts with bodies divided into three sections: head, thorax (chest) and abdomen (stomach)

nutrients food that gives living things the goodness they need to live and grow

polluted when air, water or land is poisoned or damaged

reproduce when plants and animals make young just like themselves

roots parts of a plant that grow underground. Roots take in water and goodness from the soil.

seeds these are made by a plant and released to grow into new plants

shelter somewhere safe to stay, live and have young

stem the stalk that holds up the leaves, flowers and fruit of a plant

webbed feet birds have skin between the claws of their feet. Their webbed feet are used like oars to push the water and move them along.

Index